GALE
CENGAGE Learning

Novels for Students, Volume 58

Project Editor: Kristen A. Dorsch Rights Acquisition and Management: Ashley Maynard, Carissa Poweleit Composition: Evi Abou-El-Seoud

Manufacturing: Rita Wimberley

Imaging: John Watkins

For product information and technology assistance, contact us at **Gale Customer Support, 1-800-877-4253.**

For permission to use material from this text or product, submit all requests online at **www.cengage.com/permissions**.

Further permissions questions can be emailed to **permissionrequest@cengage.com** While every effort has been made to ensure the reliability of the information presented in this publication, Gale, A Cengage Company, does not guarantee the accuracy of the data contained herein. Gale accepts no payment for listing; and inclusion in the publication of any organization, agency, institution, publication, service, or individual does not imply endorsement of the editors or publisher. Errors brought to the attention of the publisher and verified to the satisfaction of the publisher will be corrected in future editions.

Gale
27500 Drake Rd.
Farmington Hills, MI, 48331-3535

ISBN-13: 978-1-4103-6557-6
ISSN 1094-3552

This title is also available as an e-book.
ISBN-13: 978-1-4103-9286-2
ISBN-10: 1-4103-9286-2
Contact your Gale, A Cengage Company sales

representative for ordering information.

Printed in Mexico
1 2 3 4 5 6 7 22 21 20 19 18

All the Light We Cannot See

Anthony Doerr

2014

Introduction

All the Light We Cannot See is a historical novel published in 2014 by American author Anthony Doerr. The novel was both a critical and a commercial success. In 2015 it won both the Pulitzer Prize for Fiction and the Andrew Carnegie Medal for Excellence in Fiction. It reached number one on the *New York Times* best-seller list in early 2015 and remained on the best-seller list for 134 weeks.

The novel is set largely during World War II, although its final two parts reach ahead to 1974, then to 2014. It focuses on two young people caught up in the war. One is Marie-Laure Le-Blanc, the blind daughter of a locksmith at the Museum of Natural History in Paris. After the Nazi invasion of France, she and her father flee to the walled town of Saint-Malo on the coast of Brittany, where they live with her eccentric great-uncle. Meanwhile, Werner Pfennig is a white-haired orphan living in an orphanage in Germany. He has a gift for science and math and particularly for fixing broken radios, earning him admission to an elite Nazi training school. His job in the war is to hunt down contraband radios used by resistance fighters. The paths of the two characters converge in 1944, when the Allies bomb Saint-Malo. Meanwhile, Marie-Laure's father is entrusted with a mysterious—and possibly cursed—blue diamond from the Museum of Natural History, which he takes to Saint-Malo and hides in a wooden model he makes of Saint-Malo and the great-uncle's house. This gem, the Sea of Flames, becomes the target of a hunt conducted by an evil Nazi gemologist.

Doerr has commented on the origins of *All the Light We Cannot See*, which took him ten years to write and which he wove together out of bits and pieces of experience. The first occurred in 2003, when he overheard a conversation in which a man was complaining about cell phone coverage, triggering the idea of a boy listening to a radio. A second took place the following year, when he traveled to Saint-Malo in France to promote his book *About Grace*. In the past, the city, perched on a rocky coast, was populated by pirates, who often hid in deep cellars; the Allied bombing of Saint-Malo in this way became a focal point for the novel. He then read an article about how curators at the Iraqi National Museum in Baghdad had hidden the museum's treasures to safeguard them from looters and possible damage during the Iraq War of the early 2000s, giving him the idea of the gem housed at the museum in Paris but later spirited away and hidden. Doerr further claims that he found many of the minute details of the characters' surroundings—the objects that the characters would see and touch—in an old Sears catalog.

Author Biography

Doerr was born on October 27, 1973, in Cleveland, Ohio. His father owned a printing company; his mother was a teacher of ecology. He earned a bachelor's degree in history from Bowdoin College in Maine in 1995 and a master of fine arts degree from Bowling Green State University in Ohio in 1999. His first collection of short stories, *The Shell Collector*, was published in 2002; many of the stories are set in either Africa or New Zealand, among the places where Doerr has lived and worked. A second collection, *Memory Wall*, published in 2010, won the Story Prize in 2011. Meanwhile, his first novel, *About Grace*, was published in 2004, and a memoir, *Four Seasons in Rome: On Twins, Insomnia and the Biggest Funeral in the History of the World*, appeared in 2007. His second novel, *All the Light We Cannot See* was published in 2014 and won the Pulitzer Prize for Fiction in 2015. Doerr is also the recipient of four O. Henry Awards, three Pushcart Prizes, and a Guggenheim Fellowship. He is married and lives in Boise, Idaho, with his wife and twin sons. From 2007 to 2010 he was the Idaho writer-in-residence.

Plot Summary

All the Light We Cannot See is divided into numbered and dated chapters, from "Zero: 7 August 1944" to "Thirteen: 2014." Each of the chapters (with the exception of the very brief final one) is divided into named sections. All of these sections are brief, with some taking up less than a full page, many fewer than two. The focus of the named sections alternates between the two major characters, Marie-Laure and Werner, and the focus of the numbered chapters, until those late in the novel, alternates between the events of August 1944 and earlier years.

Zero: 7 August 1944

The novel's opening is set in Saint-Malo, France, in the final year of World War II. It introduces the reader to Marie-Laure LeBlanc, now age sixteen, and eighteen-year-old Werner Pfennig. Marie is blind and is living in the home of her great-uncle Etienne; Werner, a soldier in the German army, has been ordered to remain in a hotel called the Hotel of Bees, where the Germans have their headquarters. (The name of the hotel comes from the avocation of a long-ago owner of the building, a beekeeper.) Allied planes had dropped leaflets on the town warning its residents to evacuate. Hours later, as Allied bombers approach, Marie-Laure opens a model of the house that her father had made for her and removes a gemstone rumored to keep alive anyone who possesses it. Werner takes shelter in the cellar of the hotel. Soon bombs begin to fall.

Media Adaptations

- An unabridged audio version of *All the Light We Cannot See*, read by Zach Appelman, was released by Simon &Schuster Audio in 2014. Running time is sixteen hours and five minutes.

One: 1934

This part returns to the early childhood of Marie-Laure and Werner. Marie-Laure's father, Daniel LeBlanc, tells her about the "Sea of Flames," a supposedly cursed diamond. Later, she loses her eyesight, so she learns to negotiate the world by touch. Her father, a locksmith at the Museum of Natural History in Paris, carves a scale model of the neighborhood so that she can learn her way around based on the model. He also teaches her braille. After Germany invades France, Marie-Laure and her father prepare to evacuate Paris.

In Germany, Werner lives with a younger sister, Jutta, in an orphanage near Zollverein, a coal-mining area. One day Werner finds a broken radio and manages to fix it, enabling him and his sister to hear Nazi propaganda as well as science broadcasts. Other boys at the orphanage join the Hitler Youth, and eventually Werner is forced to join as well. He believes he will be sent to work in the coal mines, but in the meantime he enjoys repairing radios in his neighborhood. Jutta listens to forbidden foreign radio broadcasts, and in this way they learn of the bombing of Paris.

Marie-Laure and her father leave the city and travel to Saint-Malo and the home of Marie-Laure's great-uncle, Etienne. Monsieur LeBlanc is carrying with him what appears to be the Sea of Flames but may or may not be one of three replicas made by the museum director. Meanwhile, Werner escapes the coal mines when he repairs a radio for an influential man who is impressed by Werner's skills and writes a letter of recommendation that gains him admission to a special Nazi training school.

Two: 8 August 1944

The novel flashes ahead to 1944. The bombing

of Saint-Malo has begun. Werner is temporarily rendered unconscious when a bomb strikes the Hotel of Bees; after he regains consciousness, he realizes that he is injured and deafened. The cellar is demolished, trapping Werner and his companions, including one Volkheimer. Meanwhile, Etienne's house survives the bombing, and Marie-Laure makes her way from the sixth floor to a cellar beneath the kitchen.

Three: June 1940

The chapter begins by tracing the journey of Marie-Laure and her father to Saint-Malo and the home of Etienne. There they are greeted by his housekeeper, Madame Manec. As they settle in, they learn that the Germans have occupied France. After the Germans arrive in Saint-Malo, Marie-Laure remains housebound, spending time with the eccentric Etienne. He takes her to the attic to show her a radio transmitter he used to broadcast programs about science that he and his brother, Marie-Laure's grandfather, recorded years earlier (broadcasts that, ironically, Werner and Jutta had listened to). Her father meticulously measures the streets of Saint-Malo so that he can build a model of the town for his blind daughter.

The Nazis order the residents of Saint-Malo to turn in their radios; Monsieur LeBlanc and Madame Manec comply, but they do not know about the radio in the attic, where it remains hidden. Monsieur LeBlanc is summoned to Paris by museum officials, but on the way he is arrested and sent to prison; he was informed on by a nosy and suspicious neighbor when he was taking measurements of the town for his model. Before he left, however, he completed the model of Saint-Malo and hid the gem inside.

Werner undergoes a rigorous entrance exam that gains him admission to the Nazi school at Schulpforta, earning him the congratulations of his neighbors but the disdain of Jutta, who fears that the school will brutalize her brother. Werner arrives at the school, a rigid and cruel institution, where his only friend is a bunk mate named Frederick, who is later brutally beaten by another student because he is identified as the weakest among the boys. At Schulpforta, a science teacher, Dr. Hauptmann, takes note of Werner's skills and gives him special attention. The reader is introduced to a Nazi sergeant major, Reinhold von Rumpel, whose job is overseeing the confiscation of precious gems. Von Rumpel decides to track down the Sea of Flames, starting at the Paris museum, where officials show him a replica that had been stored there.

Four: 8 August 1944

Von Rumpel learns the location of Etienne's house. Werner and his fellow soldiers are trapped and try to think of a way to escape the rubble. Marie-Laure, no longer hearing any bombs, leaves the basement of the house to use the bathroom and get a drink of water. She hears someone (von Rumpel) entering the house.

Five: January 1941

Werner visits the home of Frederick's wealthy family in Berlin. When they return to the school, the students are ordered to torture to death a foreign prisoner by pouring buckets of water on him as he is tied to a stake in the snow. Frederick resists by pouring the water at his feet. Werner learns that this abuse of a prisoner is an annual ritual at the school. He and others go into the field to practice the use of trigonometry to home in on radio transmitters. One morning, Frederick, who continues to be beaten as the weakest boy, disappears. Werner learns that Frederick is having surgery and will not come back; Werner later visits him in Berlin, finding him mentally impaired by his injuries. Hauptmann, who is ordered to Berlin, lies to the government about Werner's age so that Werner can join a German military technology division.

Von Rumpel realizes that the stone he acquired at the museum is a fake. He has a medical exam, ultimately learning that he has tumors. He is now determined to find the Sea of Flames, which he believes will heal him.

Madame Manec takes Marie-Laure, who misses her father and learns that he never arrived in Paris, to the ocean, which fascinates her. As Marie-Laure makes her way to the beach each day, Madame Manec and a group of women begin to take steps to resist the Germans. They make contact with a resistance fighter, Hubert Bazin, who guides them in their efforts, although he later disappears.

After police search Etienne's home and threaten him with arrest (because of forbidden French flags), Etienne orders his housekeeper to stop conducting resistance activities from the house. Marie-Laure received a letter from her father that gives her a clue to the location of the diamond. Madame Manec contracts pneumonia, and after she recovers temporarily, she dies.

Six: 8 August 1944

Marie-Laure recognizes the sound of von Rumpel's limp; she first encountered him when Bazin took her to a secret grotto, or cave, but the narrative reveals this later, in the ninth chapter. Marie-Laure hides in the attic as von Rumpel searches the house, where he finds the model of the town and concludes that the diamond is inside. Meanwhile, one of Werner's fellow soldiers dies in the rubble of the Hotel of Bees. Werner tries to repair a damaged radio, but he can hear only static.

Seven: August 1942

Werner is part of a unit that travels about Russia searching for forbidden radio broadcasts; his job is to calculate the location of the radios so that his unit can ferret out and kill those who are sending the transmissions. He hears his first Russian rebel broadcast and leads his unit to the location, where the broadcasters are killed. By now, he has stopped writing to Jutta and rarely hears from her. After he falls ill with a fever, he directs his unit to a house in

Vienna, Austria—but it is the wrong house. His unit kills a woman and young girl in the house, even though they do not have a radio.

Etienne and Marie-Laure decide to carry out Madame Manec's plans of resistance. For several months, they broadcast coded resistance messages that are baked into loaves of bread they get from a nearby bakery. They also broadcast messages from people in the community who are trying to locate friends and loved ones. Using intelligence Etienne has transmitted, French resistance fighters destroy a bridge, killing a number of German soldiers. A German commander requests help in locating a radio in or near Saint-Malo—Etienne's radio.

In the process of valuing gems seized from Polish Jews, von Rumpel comes across a second Sea of Flames replica. Later, he finds a third. He reasons that the genuine stone had to have been in the possession of the museum's locksmith, Monsieur LeBlanc. In the LeBlanc apartment in Paris, he finds the father's model of the apartment and destroys it to determine whether the diamond is inside.

Eight: 9 August 1944

Saint-Malo is again under bombardment. Marie-Laure finds a braille copy of Jules Verne's *Twenty Thousand Leagues under the Sea* and takes it with her to the attic, where she decides to broadcast herself reading aloud from the book. Werner, meanwhile, continues to pick up only static from the radio he has tried to repair in the cellar of the Hotel of Bees—until he suddenly hears the voice of Marie-Laure reading the book. Von Rumpel is in the house, and Werner hears Marie-Laure whisper, "He is here. He is right below me." Werner resolves to help her.

Nine: May 1944

Werner and his unit travel to France in an effort to locate Etienne's radio; he recognizes Etienne's voice from the long-ago radio broadcasts. When the unit arrives in Saint-Malo, Werner spots an antenna on the chimney of Etienne's house. He sees Marie-Laure as she is leaving the house. In the weeks that follow, Werner continues to think about Marie-Laure and wants to save her, but he worries that trying to do so will endanger him. He then sees the Allied plane that drops leaflets over the city, warning the residents to evacuate; the narrative has now arrived at the events of early August depicted in "Zero: 7 August 1944."

Meanwhile, in May, Marie-Laure learns that the Allies are planning to invade France. At the grotto, she has an encounter with von Rumpel, who has only months to live and who has learned of the arrest of Marie-Laure's father. He questions Marie-Laure about the Sea of Flames, prompting her to find the gem in a model her father made of Etienne's house. Etienne is arrested when he is caught outside after curfew, trying to map the locations of German antiaircraft guns for the Allies. Marie-Laure refuses to evacuate the city.

Ten: 12 August 1944

Marie-Laure continues to broadcast *Twenty Thousand Leagues under the Sea*, and Werner continues to listen. When she is done, Werner feels hopeless. He and his companion in the cellar, Volkheimer, use a grenade to blast a hole through a wall, allowing them to escape. Werner goes to Etienne's house to rescue Marie-Laure. As he is climbing to the attic, he has an encounter with von Rumpel and shoots him. He finally meets Marie-Laure, and the two share a can of peaches. After the bombardment stops, the two evacuate the city, but not before Marie-Laure hides the Sea of Flames in the grotto, leaving the key to the grotto's gate with Werner. The two part ways: Marie-Laure is reunited with Etienne, and Werner, after being arrested by the Allies, wanders into a minefield and is killed.

Eleven: 1945

As the war is drawing to a close, Jutta and other girls from the orphanage, along with Frau Elena, who runs the orphanage, are made to work in a factory in Berlin. They know that the Russians are approaching, and their fears of Russian brutality are borne out when Russian soldiers rape them. Jutta later becomes a math teacher. Etienne and Marie-Laure move to the Paris apartment that she once lived in with her father. They continue to try to find Monsieur LeBlanc, hoping that he was released from the German prison where he was held; in fact, he died in 1943.

Twelve: 1974

Nearly three decades later, Volk heimer is contacted by an organization that is trying to return the belongings of dead soldiers to their families. The organization has found Werner's belongings and the wooden model of the house in Saint-Malo, which Volkheimer takes to Jutta. He tells Jutta that he believes Werner fell in love in Saint-Malo. Jutta travels to Saint-Malo with her son, where she learns Marie-Laure's address in Paris. She then travels to Paris, where she finds Marie-Laure working in the Museum of Natural History. She gives Marie-Laure the model of the house, in which she finds the key to the grotto, where Werner had left the Sea of Flames.

Thirteen: 2014

Marie-Laure, now in her eighties, is at a park with her grandson while he plays a computer game. She tells the boy that for her twelfth birthday, she wanted a copy of *Twenty Thousand Leagues under the Sea*. She wonders whether all the electromagnetic waves surrounding her contain the souls of her loved ones and whether she could hear them. She walks home with her grandson, where she stands outside listening to the sounds of the world around her.

Characters

All the Light We Cannot See has a large cast of characters, including more than two dozen named but minor characters. This list names the characters who play larger roles in the narrative.

Hubert Bazin

Hubert is a fighter in the French Resistance. He gives Marie-Laure the key to the grotto gate, where the Sea of Flames is ultimately hidden.

Frau Elena

Frau Elena is the director of the orphanage in which Werner and Jutta grow up.

Frederick

Frederick is Werner Pfennig's friend and bunk mate at the training school at Schulpforta. Because he is identified by the other students as the weakest among them, especially after refusing to torture an enemy prisoner, he is mercilessly beaten, leaving him disabled.

Doctor Hauptmann

Hauptmann is a teacher at the training school at Schulpforta. Having discovered Werner Pfennig's technical skills, he gives Werner special attention and gets him assigned to the German military.

Daniel LeBlanc

Daniel, Marie-Laure's father, works as a locksmith at the Museum of Natural History in Paris. Skilled with his hands, he builds a model of their Paris neighborhood so that his blind daughter can learn to navigate it. When the two evacuate Paris after the German invasion, he takes with him a valuable diamond called the Sea of Flames. At Etienne's house in Saint-Malo, he hides the diamond in a wooden model of the house. He is later arrested by the Germans and sent to prison, where he dies in 1943.

Etienne LeBlanc

Etienne is Marie-Laure's great-uncle, the brother of her grandfather. Etienne has been traumatized by his service in World War I and finds it difficult to leave his house in Saint-Malo, although his love for Marie-Laure helps to restore him. In his attic is an old radio that he and his now-deceased brother set up years earlier to broadcast science programs. He and Marie-Laure use the radio to transmit intelligence from the French Resistance to the Allies.

Marie-Laure LeBlanc

Marie-Laure, the daughter of a locksmith at the

Museum of Natural History in Paris, goes blind at the age of six. Accordingly, she learns to navigate her world by sound and touch. She and her father evacuate Paris after the German invasion of France and move in with her great-uncle, Etienne, in Saint-Malo, a walled city on the coast of Brittany. During the war years, she and her great-uncle use an old radio transmitter to make prohibited broadcasts and to help the French Resistance. In 1944, when she is age sixteen, she is trapped inside the house during the Allied bombardment of the city. Her father has hidden a valuable diamond in a model of the house he has constructed for her. Ultimately, she and the radio are located by Werner, a German soldier, and the two evacuate the city. After the war, she works at the museum where her father worked and gives birth to a daughter.

Madame Manec

Madame Manec is Etienne's housekeeper. She and a number of elderly women in Saint-Malo decide to work for the French Resistance, arranging for information to be sent to her hidden in loaves of bread. She dies before she can persuade Etienne to let her use the radio in the attic to transmit intelligence to the Allies.

Jutta Pfennig

Jutta is Werner Pfennig's sister. At the orphanage where she lives with her brother, she listens to foreign radio broadcasts, making her skeptical of Nazi propaganda. She does not want Werner to attend the training school in Schulpforta, believing that the training will brutalize him. After the war, she is raped by Russian soldiers occupying Berlin, and she later becomes a math teacher.

Werner Pfennig

Werner grows up in an orphanage in Germany. It is discovered that he has great technical skills, particularly in repairing radios. He is sent to an elite Nazi training school at Schulpforta and ultimately drafted into the military, where his job is to use his technical skills to locate illegal radios. After he picks up a broadcast from Saint-Malo, he locates the house where Marie-Laure is living. He is stationed at the German headquarters in the Hotel of Bees, but when the Allies bomb the city in August 1944, he is trapped in the rubble of a cellar. He escapes, rescues Marie-Laure from the clutches of von Rumpel, a Nazi gem hunter, and dies as a prisoner of war.

Volkheimer

Volkheimer attends the training school at Schulpforta with Werner Pfennig and ultimately becomes a member of Werner's unit. He is trapped with Werner in the cellar of the Hotel of Bees in Saint-Malo after the Allied bombardment.

Reinhold von Rumpel

Von Rumpel, a sergeant major in the German army, is a gemologist; his job is to acquire and value confiscated gems. He devotes much of his effort to locating the Sea of Flames diamond, believing in the legend that the diamond makes its possessor immortal. He pursues the diamond to Saint-Malo and Etienne's house, where he is killed by Werner Pfennig.

War

All the Light We Cannot See is first and foremost a war novel, focusing on the effects of World War II on its characters. The focal point of the novel—the end point to which its narrative arc leads—is the bombing by British and American planes of Saint-Malo, a walled town on the Brittany coast of northwestern France. The key events that lead to this climax take place in the years leading up to it. In the 1930s, Marie-Laure LeBlanc and her father would have watched the resurgence of Germany after its humiliation by the Treaty of Versailles, which ended World War I. Adolf Hitler, the German dictator, escalated his territorial demands in Europe until he invaded France, forcing Marie-Laure and her father to evacuate Paris and take up residence in Saint-Malo.

Meanwhile, Werner Pfennig is caught up in the fervor of Nazism, attends an elite military training school, and is assigned to a technology unit tasked with the responsibility of hunting down forbidden radios and their owners. Initially, Werner buys into the propaganda disseminated by the Nazi regime, but as the war progresses, he becomes increasingly disillusioned by the barbarity of his Nazi overlords and is determined to come to the aid of Marie-Laure. The novel, however, does not enter into geopolitical or philosophical analysis of the war. Rather, it focuses on the consequences of war as it affects individuals and families, who find ways to survive, if they can, in spite of the insanity around them.

Nazism

Perhaps one of the most extraordinary developments of the twentieth century was the rapid rise of the National Socialist Party in post–World War I Germany and its ability to sweep up the German population in right-wing, nationalistic, militaristic, anti-Communist, and anti-Semitic fervor. The term *Nazi* is a collapsed form of the German-language name of the party and its ideology, *Nationalsozialismus*. The party began as the German Workers' Party, which grew in size and influence as the postwar Weimar Republic was unable to improve Germany's economic conditions or to curb the rampant lawlessness that arose from clashes between right-wing and left-wing factions vying for control. Out of this chaos, a relatively obscure figure, Adolf Hitler, seized power and consolidated it through a combination of violence, symbolism, propaganda, and an ability to give captivating, emotional speeches.

Hitler and the Nazi hierarchy believed that the future of a strong, dominant, racially superior state lay with Germany's youth. Accordingly, they fostered the Hitler Jugend, or Hitler Youth movement, which Werner, having little choice, joins in Doerr's novel. When Hitler began his rise to power, membership in the Hitler Youth stood at about one hundred thousand, but by 1936 the movement included four million members, and it was virtually required that all boys join. At age ten, boys joined the Deutsches Jungvolk, or German Young People; at age thirteen, they moved to the Hitlerjugend, or Hitler Youth, where they remained until age eighteen. The emphasis in the movement was on toughness, both physical and mental, in preparation for military service. Accordingly, boys practiced martial skills, such as marching, shooting, map reading, and the like. Meanwhile, girls at age ten joined the Jungmädelbund, or League of Young Girls; at age fourteen, they moved to the Bund Deutscher Mädel, or League of German Girls. Again, the emphasis was on physical strength with a view to training girls to become mothers of Germany's next generation of "racially superior" stock.

Topics for Further Study

- Conduct research into World War II, specifically, the German occupation of France and other nations of western Europe, the establishment of Vichy France, and Allied bombing campaigns conducted in an effort to liberate France and other nations. Present the results of your investigation in an oral report to your classmates.

- Locate online or in print a map of western Europe from late in World War II. Using a tech tool such as Jing.com, share your map with your classmates and explain to them the key events of the war that play a role in *All the Light We Cannot See*.

- For centuries, stories have circulated about rare and valuable gems—gems that are also cursed. Conduct research into cursed diamonds, rubies, sapphires, and other gems similar to the Sea of Flames in Doerr's novel. Settle on one that particularly interests you and write your own short story about it and how it affects the lives of people who come in contact with it. Share your story with your classmates on your social media site and invite them to comment.

- A novel that revolves around the disappearance of a mysterious gemstone is Wilkie Collins's *The Moonstone* (Barnes and Noble Classics, 2005), first published in 1868. Read the novel, then write a brief report about Collins's use of the gemstone to advance his story, contrasting it with Doerr's.

- *Code Name Verity* (Hyperion, 2012), by Elizabeth Wein, is a sometimes intense novel written for mature teens about the horrors of World War II and the Resistance in France. Like *All the Light We Cannot See*, it features strong female characters. Read the novel, then imagine a dialogue between "Verity" and Marie-Laure from Doerr's novel. With a willing classmate, perform your dialog for your classmates.

- *Mare's War* (Knopf, 2007), by Tanita S. Davis, features a modern-day grandmother telling her granddaughters about her experiences during World War II as a black woman in the segregated Women's Army Corps unit in Europe. Read the novel, then imagine yourself as one of its characters writing a letter home about life in an all-black women's unit in Europe. Share your letter with your classmates and invite them to comment.

- As World War II seemed imminent, museums in Paris and other European cities moved their collections to safe locations, both to protect them from potential bombing damage and to keep them out of the clutches of the Nazis. What specific steps did such museums as the Museum of Natural History or the Louvre take? Did other museums in Europe take similar steps? Present the results of your investigation in an oral report to your classmates.

Fate

All the Light We Cannot See takes on the issue of fate and the usually unpredictable circumstances that enable people to cross paths as events around them lead them to a time and place. From the first chapter, which is set in Saint-Malo in August 1944, the reader knows that Marie-Laure and Werner will be brought together—that their paths will cross in a way that brings their stories to a conclusion. The remainder of the novel, then, alternates between events that take place during that month, as the Allies bomb the city, and the backstory that leads the two characters there. The reader experiences a constant sense of dramatic irony, watching as historical events lead the characters to their mutual destinies.

On this level, the novel raises the question of whether characters have any control over what happens to them. The paths of Marie-Laure and Werner lead them to the city, but when the bombs start to fall, they are essentially helpless. The reader is left asking whether people can make choices in wartime and whether different choices might lead to different outcomes: Marie-Laure, for example, could have chosen to evacuate Saint-Malo in response to the leaflets the Allies dropped. Because of the strictures of the Nazi regime, Werner would seem to have less control over his fate. Ultimately, the novel raises the question of whether one's fate is predetermined or whether the individual can exert control over it.

Structure

All the Light We Cannot See employs an unusual narrative structure, for the novel consists in large part of *two* narrative arcs that come together near the end. The author alternates these narratives, so that one named section that focuses on Marie-Laure is followed by another named section that focuses on Werner. In essence, the two narrative arcs have little to do with each other, although the author hints at connections: Perhaps the most significant has to do with radios. Werner is conversant with radios, and during the war his job is to track down unauthorized radios and radio broadcasts; meanwhile, a forbidden radio is in Etienne's attic, and he and Marie-Laure send out broadcasts. Additionally, Werner and his sister listened to the recordings of science broadcasts Etienne and his brother made years earlier and that Etienne rebroadcasts later. Otherwise, the narratives have little overlap.

Also unusual is the alternation between time periods. One section of the novel focuses on the events of the 1930s or the early years of the war, but the following section focuses on August 1944 and the bombing of Saint-Malo. This back-and-forth pattern serves multiple purposes. If the central events of the novel take place in August 1944, then the other sections provide backstory, informing the reader of how the characters arrived in the position they are in. Further, the structure creates a great deal of dramatic irony: Because of the 1944 sections, the reader knows the outcome of events in a way that the characters, of course, do not as their fates unfold. This heightens the sense of anticipation as the paths of Marie-Laure and Werner eventually meet.

Dramatic Irony

Dramatic irony is a literary device by which the viewer (of a play or movie) or a reader (of a work of fiction) has a broader understanding of events or characters than that of the characters themselves. Dramatic irony is a common device authors use to heighten the tension of a work or to engage the interest, sympathy, or involvement of the audience/reader in the events depicted. Because of the structure of *All the Light We Cannot See*, with its alternation between the events of August 1944 and those that took place in the years leading up to that point, the reader gains insight into the backstory of the characters in a way that involves the reader in the construction of the story. The novel is rife with dramatic irony, but one example perhaps illustrates the point. Marie-Laure's great-uncle, Etienne, describes to her the radio shows about science that he and his brother recorded years earlier, but he indicates that he does not know whether anyone ever heard them. The reader, however, knows that Werner and Jutta listened to them and found them a source of inspiration. The irony is that Etienne's broadcasts on what would become a forbidden radio transmitter in part lead Werner to the house in Saint-Malo and to Marie-Laure.

Historical Context

The bulk of *All the Light We Cannot See* takes place between the years 1934 and 1945, with the focal point being the Allied bombing of Saint-Malo in 1944. In the 1930s, most of the people of France would have looked on with unease as a resurgent Germany was repudiating the terms of the Treaty of Versailles by rearming and beginning to flex its muscles in Europe. In 1933, a relatively unknown Adolf Hitler became chancellor of Germany. In the months that followed, Hitler consolidated his power by banning the Communist Party, eliminating trade unions, withdrawing from the League of Nations, and crushing opposition within his own National Socialist (Nazi) Party.

In August 1934, in response to the death of the president of Germany, Paul von Hindenburg, Hitler named himself Führer and Reich chancellor, eliminating the position of president. Over the next four years, Hitler rattled his sabers, escalating his demands for territory as the rest of Europe— unwilling to endure another major war on its soil after the horrors of World War I—capitulated. Virtually everyone in Germany was swept up in Nazi fervor. Young people, such as Werner Pfennig, were recruited to serve the state, and the Hitler Youth movement indoctrinated teenage boys in the principles and attitudes of National Socialism.

World War II officially began on September 1,

1939, with the German invasion of Poland. In 1940, Hitler's forces invaded Denmark, Norway, Belgium, and the Netherlands, and on June 14, 1940, the German army marched into Paris. In effect, the German invasion divided France in half. After France signed an armistice with Germany on June 22, 1940, the German military occupied the northern portion of the country, including Paris, which remained the de jure capital of France. The southern portion of the country was an unoccupied, nominally "free zone" whose de facto capital was Vichy. The official ideology of this region, under the command of Marshal Henri Philippe Pétain, was authoritarian and right wing. Still in the twenty-first century, "Vichy France" is held in revulsion for its collaboration with the Nazis, including its role in the Holocaust against Jews in France. In late 1942, after Allied forces landed in North Africa, Hitler ordered his forces to occupy the southern zone of France.

The division in France was a reflection of ideological divisions that beset the nation during the years of Marie-Laure's childhood (she is six years old in 1934). The 1930s were a period of instability for France. The onset of the worldwide Great Depression boosted the appeal of extremist groups on both the left and the right. On the right, those whose roots extended to the traditional French aristocracy and who were never able to accept the principles of the French Revolution—liberty, equality, and fraternity—were drawn to fascism. In many cases, they were happy to see Hitler's successes. On the left, workers and others were drawn to communism. In 1934 a series of riots pitting left against right exposed the weaknesses of the French government. Then in 1936, Leon Blum, a Jew, became prime minister, and in that year's elections the leftist Popular Front emerged victorious. These developments further inflamed the nation's conservative, anti-Semitic right wing, but just a year later, the Popular Front government collapsed, to be replaced by a rightist government. This social and political turmoil contributed to France's inability—or unwillingness—to effectively resist Hitler.

By 1944, Hitler knew he was in trouble. The Allies had successfully landed troops on the beaches of Normandy on D-day, June 6, 1944. Hitler ordered that various cities in France be regarded as *Festungen*, or fortresses, where German units were to use any means possible to impede the Allied advance through France—and where surrender was not an option. One region of France the Allies wanted to reclaim was Brittany, on the English Channel in northwestern France. The Germans maintained a number of naval bases there, including U-boat stations, and the Allies knew that gaining the upper hand in the English Channel required the elimination of these bases.

One of the *Festungen* of Brittany was Saint-Malo, a walled city with a complex of underground caverns that is perched right on the coast. Although details are disputed, it is believed that the French Resistance informed American commanders that as many as ten thousand German troops occupied the city. The German commander of Saint-Malo, General Andreas von Aulock, refused to surrender to the Allies, and in an Allied bombing and shelling campaign that began in late August and continued into September 1944, the city was almost totally destroyed. It has since been rebuilt.

Critical Overview

All the Light We Cannot See, which won the Pulitzer Prize for Fiction in 2015, met with a groundswell of critical approval. A *Publishers Weekly* critic comments: "If a book's success can be measured by its ability to move readers and the number of memorable characters it has … Doerr's novel triumphs on both counts." John Freeman, writing for the *Boston Globe*, calls the novel "remarkable" and observes that it "reflects a dazzling array of themes" and that its language is "startlingly fresh." Amanda Vaill, in a review for the *Washington Post*, finds the novel "enthral-lingly told, beautifully written and so emotionally plangent that some passages bring tears." Vaill further comments:

> Cutting back and forth in time, he creates nearly unbearable suspense. Every piece of back story reveals information that charges the emerging narrative with significance, until at last the puzzle-box of the plot slides open to reveal the treasure hidden inside.

Equally enthusiastic is Steph Cha of the *Los Angeles Times*, who terms the novel "a beautiful, expansive tale, woven with thoughtful reflections on the meaning of life, the universe and everything." Cha, who praises the novel as "ambitious" and "majestic" and who finds its prose "wondrous" and "magical," remarks on the significant of the title:

> The title refers to the endless run of the electromagnetic spectrum, a scale so large that "mathematically, all of light is invisible." This motif runs through the whole novel, imparting texture and rhythm as well as a thematic tension, between the insignificant and miraculous natures of mankind and all the immeasurable components that make up our lives.

Compare & Contrast

- **1944:** The United States and its allies are at war with Nazi Germany and have gained a foothold in France with the Normandy invasion on D-day in June.

  Today: The United States and its allies carry out military missions in the Middle East in the ongoing war against terrorism.

- **1944:** Germany is still under the firm control of dictator Adolf Hitler and the Nazi Party, although its military has suffered setbacks and is on the defensive.

  Today: Germany is a democratic nation and, along with France, is a US ally, a member of the North

Atlantic Treaty Organization (NATO), and a member of the European Union.

- **1944:** Much of Saint-Malo, France, is destroyed when the city is bombed by Allied forces in an effort to regain control of the English Channel and of French ports.
  Today: Saint-Malo, France, has been rebuilt, and the walled city is a tourist attraction in Brittany.

Writing for the *New York Times*, Janet Maslin pronounces the novel "hauntingly beautiful," "surprisingly fresh and enveloping," and "intricate" and praises it for its "acutely sensory style." Yvonne Zipp, in a review for the *Christian Science Monitor*, calls the novel "deeply moral" and Doerr's "best work to date." Zipp notes: "There are certain tropes that have perhaps been overdone in literature: orphans, plucky children with a disability, cursed gemstones, World War II. Anthony Doerr combines all of the above …and pulls it off with stylistic aplomb."

Not all critics were as laudatory. William T. Vollmann, also writing for the *New York Times*, seems of two minds about the novel. On one hand, he writes that "Marie-Laure is an exquisitely realized creation." On the other he points out that the novel

falls shortest when it tries to deal

with Nazism. It falls back on flimsy types. Frederick is one. At times Werner is another. Most preposterous of all is a certain Sgt. Maj. Reinhold von Rumpel, whose wickedness and physical loathsomeness are offset by nothing that could make him into a rounded character.

Similarly, Vollmann offers muted praise by remarking that "the book contains enough flashes of real talent that I kept hoping for more than entertainment. When he takes the trouble, Doerr can write beautifully, both page for page and line for line."

One critic who found fault with the novel was Dominic Green of *New Republic*. Characterizing the novel as the "impeccably implausible tale of two children," Green complains that "the plot grinds toward the meeting of Werner and Marie-Laure with the subtlety of a Tiger tank." He further disparages the "twee sentiment" of the novel's ending and feels that "Doerr's writing is pompous, pretentious, and imprecise. Every noun is escorted by an adjective of reliable but uninspiring quality." Commenting on what he saw as the novel's false and misleading depiction of history, Green notes: "As a relativizer, [Doerr] presents all violence, Nazi or Allied, as equivalent: the product of amoral, deterministic forces." Green objects that this might add to the "aesthetic value" of the novel but at the same time "might dumb the moral sense." In the same vein, Green observes that "when World War II is reduced to a conflict between technological determinism and innocent children, the difference between aggressors and defenders is erased."

What Do I Read Next?

- *About Grace* (Scribner, 2004), Doerr's first novel, tells the story of a man who has disturbing visions of the future and tries desperately to escape them.

- *The Children's War* (Thorndike Press, 2004), by Monique Charlesworth, bears a number of similarities to *All the Light We Cannot See*. Set in World War II, the novel weaves together the stories of Ilse, a half-Jewish girl whose mother sends her away from Germany to her safety, and Nicolai, a German boy who is a member of the Hitler Youth.

- *Girl in the Blue Coat* (Little, Brown, 2016) is a young-adult novel set in Nazi-occupied Holland during World War II. The protagonist is Hanneke, a black market courier who lost her boyfriend in battle during the German invasion of Holland.

- *The Girl in the Blue Beret* (Random House, 2011), by Bobbie Ann Mason, is a novel that tells the story of an American pilot shot down over Belgium in 1944. With the help of Belgian and French citizens, he manages to escape the Nazis. Years later, he returns to the site of the crash and tries to find "the girl in the blue beret" who came to his aid.

- Readers interested in the experience of African Americans during World War II might start with Maggi Morehouse's *Fighting in the Jim Crow Army: Black Men and Women Remember World War II* (Rowman & Littlefield, 2000).

- *World War II* (DK, 2008), by R. G. Grant, is a lavishly illustrated volume that presents younger readers with a comprehensive history of World War II, including the circumstances that led to the war, its major battles, and its consequences.

- Robert Gildea's *Fighters in the Shadows: A New History of the French Resistance* (Har-vard University Press, 2015) tells the story of the French Resistance in a way that strips away some of the mythology that has grown up around it.

- *And There Was Light: The Extraordinary Memoir of a Blind Hero of the French Resistance in World War II* (New World Library, 2014) is Jacques Lusseyran's memoir about his experiences as a blind leader of a Resistance group in Paris during World War II. Doerr cites the memoir as having in part inspired *All the Light We Cannot See*.

Sources

Cha, Steph, Review of *All the Light We Cannot See*, in *Los Angeles Times*, May 23, 2014, http://www.latimes.com/books/jacketcopy/la-ca-jc-anthony-doerr-20140525-story.html (accessed August 5, 2017).

Doerr, Anthony, *All the Light We Cannot See*, Scribner, 2014.

Ferguson, Julie H., "St. Malo, France: Then and Now," Europe Up Close, April 19, 2017, https://europeupclose.com/article/st-malo-france/ (accessed August 18, 2017).

Freeman, John, Review of *All the Light We Cannot See*, in *Boston Globe*, May 3, 2014, https://www.bostonglobe.com/arts/books/2014/05/0: all-light-cannot-see-anthony-doerr/BCqWZuK73k2ZkdAtkhyt9L/story.html (August 14, 2017).

Green, Dominic, "One-Armed Nazis and Albino Children: The Year's Surprise Bestseller Turns the Holocaust into a Sentimental Mess," Review of *All the Light We Cannot See*, in *New Republic*, January 14, 2015, https://newrepublic.com/article/120769/problem-anthony-doerrs-all-light-we-cannot-see (accessed August 5, 2017).

"Hitler's Rise and Fall: Timeline," OpenLearn, July 18, 2017, http://www.open.edu/openlearn/history-the-arts/history/hitlers-rise-and-fall-timeline (accessed August 7, 2017).

Maslin, Janet, "Light Found in Darkness of Wartime," Review of *All the Light We Cannot See*, in *New York Times*, April 9, 2014, p. C1.

Review of *All the Light We Cannot See*, in *Publishers Weekly*, https://www.publishersweekly.com/978-1-4767-4658-6 (accessed August 5, 2017).

"The Rise of the Nazi Party," Florida Center for Instructional Technology, College of Education, University of South Florida, 2005, http://fcit.usf.edu/holocaust/TIMELINE/nazirise.HT (accessed August 14, 2017).

Schulman, Martha, "How the Story Comes Together: Anthony Doerr," in *Publishers Weekly*, April 11, 2014, https://www.publishersweekly.com/pw/by-topic/authors/profiles/article/61823-how-the-story-comes-together-anthony-doerr.html (accessed August 5, 2017).

Simkin, John, "Vichy France," Spartacus Educational, September 1997, http://spartacus-educational.com/2WWvichy.htm (accessed August 7, 2017).

Trueman, C. N. "The Battle for Brittany," History Learning Site, April 20, 2015, http://www.historylearningsite.co.uk/world-war-two/world-war-two-in-western-europe/the-battle-for-brittany/ (accessed August 7, 2017).

————, "Hitler Youth Movement," History Learning Site, March 9, 2015, http://www.historylearningsite.co.uk/nazi-germany/hitler-youth-movement/ (accessed August 14, 2017).

Vaill, Amanda, Review of *All the Light We Cannot See*, in *Washington Post*, May 5, 2014, https://www.washingtonpost.com/entertainment/boo the-light-we-cannot-see-by-anthony-doerr/2014/05/05/c2deec58-cf14-11e3-a6b1-45c4dffb85a6_story.html?utm_term=.7720c776d026 (accessed August 5, 2017).

Vollmann, William T., "Darkness Visible," Review of *All the Light We Cannot See*, in *New York Times*, May 11, 2014, p. BR16.

Zipp, Yvonne, "'All the Light We Cannot See' Is a Compelling WWII Novel by Acclaimed Author Anthony Doerr," in *Christian Science Monitor*, May 21, 2014, https://www.csmonitor.com/Books/Book-Reviews/2014/0521/All-the-Light-We-Cannot-See-is-a-compelling-WWII-novel-by-acclaimed-author-Anthony-Doerr (accessed August 7, 2017).

Further Reading

Chanel, Gerri, *Saving Mona Lisa: The Battle to Protect the Louvre and Its Treasures during World War II*, Heliopa Press, 2014.

> In August 1939, as German forces were nearing Paris, curators at the Louvre in Paris shipped what is perhaps its most famous painting, the *Mona Lisa*, to the Loire valley to protect it from Hitler's henchmen. Other masterpieces were similarly spirited away. This volume recreates the story of the immense responsibility borne by those driven by a desire to preserve the nation's cultural inheritance, often risking their lives in doing so.

Cobb, Matthew, *The Resistance: The French Fight against the Nazis*, Simon &Schuster UK, 2013.

> Cobb's book is based on hundreds of eyewitness accounts and on newly released archival material. These personal stories give the reader access to one of the great stories of heroism and survival in the twentieth century.

Dodd, Lindsey, *French Children under the Allied Bombs, 1940–45: An Oral History*, Manchester

University Press, 2016.

An entry in the publishers Cultural History of Modern War series, this volume looks at the Allied bombing of France, which may have killed as many as fifty-seven thousand civilians, from the perspective of children. Through oral histories, it provides insight into civilian life, particularly in Vichy France.

Hyslop, Stephen, and Neil Kagan, eds., *Eyewitness to World War II: Unforgettable Stories and Photographs from History's Greatest Conflict*, National Geographic, 2012.

This volume includes first-person accounts of World War II from those who lived through it, both at home and on the battlefield. It features materials written by such historical figures as Franklin D. Roosevelt, Adolf Hitler, and General George Patton, as well as letters written by soldiers and diaries written by women who served in the military.

Suggested Search Terms

All the Light We Cannot See Allied bombing AND France AND World War II Anthony Doerr

children in Nazi Germany German occupation of France Hitler Youth

National Museum of Natural History France OR Muséum national d'Histoire naturelle Saint-Malo AND history World War II AND Europe AND resistance movements

Lightning Source UK Ltd.
Milton Keynes UK
UKHW021916080120
356598UK00018B/245/P